21st CENTURY CLARINET SERIES

FOUR SHORT PIECES

Frank Bridge

Arranged for Clarinet and Piano by

Paula Corley

PIANO

keisersouthernmusic.com

PERFORMANCE NOTES

Frank Bridge was born in February of 1879 in Brighton, England. He began his musical life as a violinist, at London's Royal College of Music. Later he switched to the viola and became known as a virtuoso on the instrument as well as a composer and teacher. His catalogue of works contains 192 compositions written between 1900 and 1941. One of his private composition students was Benjamin Britten with whom he maintained a close friendship. In 1939, shortly before his death, he gifted Britten with his Giussani viola.

Four Short Pieces was composed in 1912 and was originally written for violin or cello with piano. A number of recordings exist for these combinations as well as a version for flute and piano. This arrangement for clarinet and piano follows the original closely with regards to tempo, style and articulation. Markings are suggested and the performer is encouraged to make adjustments to facilitate musicality.

Ranges

Movement one, *Meditation*, is an elegant and lyrical ABA form that showcases the chalumeau and clarion register of the clarinet. The peaceful opening quickly changes to a more intense *piu mosso* at ms. 19 before ending quietly.

Spring Song is a quick, up-tempo melody in 2/4 that is reminiscent of a brisk walk or carriage ride in the English countryside. The style is legato and there are some large interval skips.

Lullaby is a slow waltz that requires good air support as the clarinetist must sustain with a beautiful sound throughout.

Country Dance is the most technically demanding of the movements in quick 6/8 time. The clarinetist must move fluidly through the full range of the instrument while creating the "dance" style through carefully placed agogic accents. The accents should be substantial, and both clarinetist and pianist should work for contrast when they appear.

Four Short Pieces

I. Meditation

Frank Bridge
arranged by Paula Corley

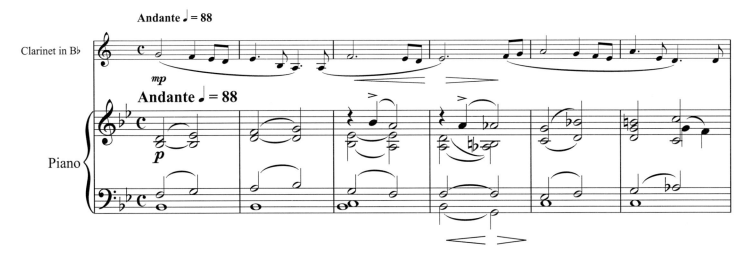

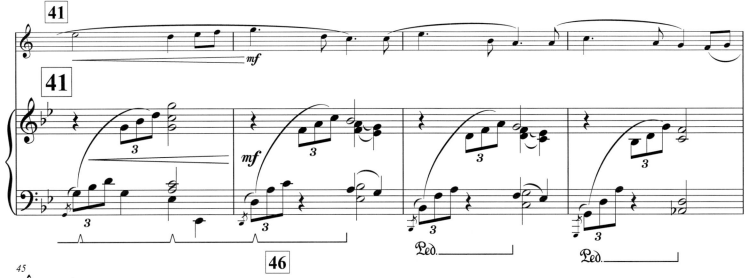

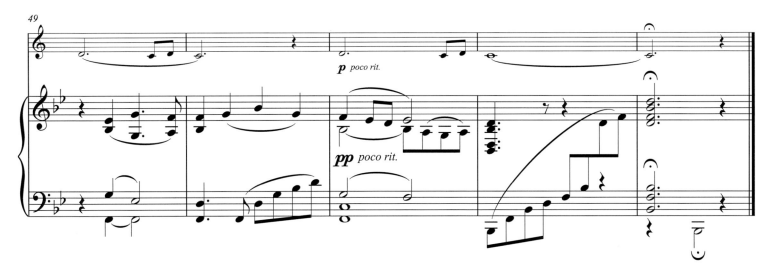

II. Spring Song

Frank Bridge
arranged by Paula Corley

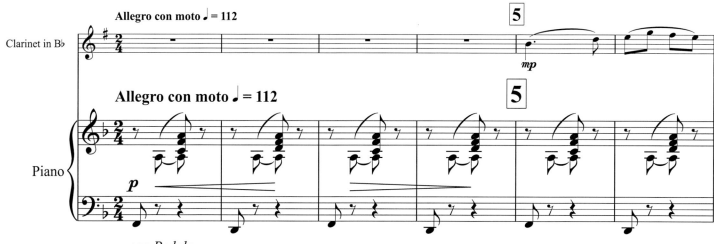

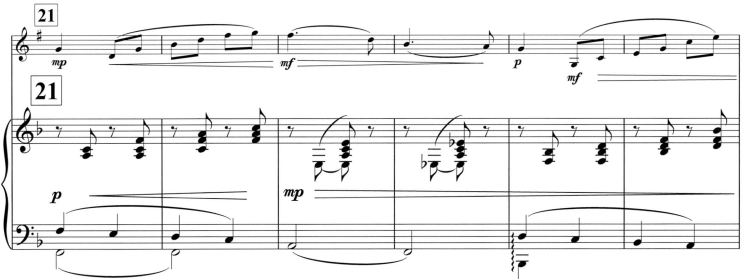

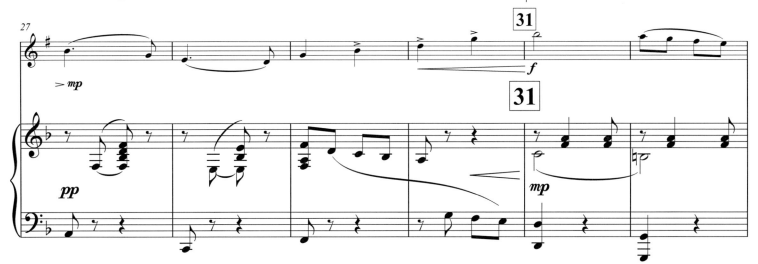

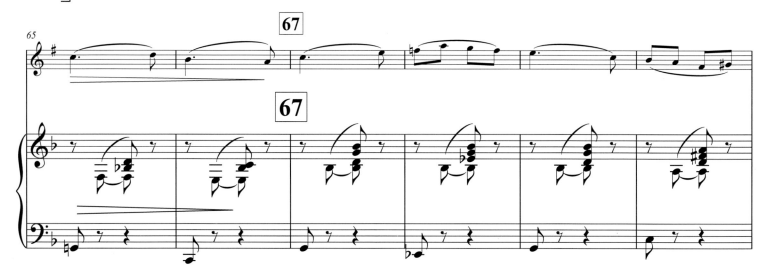

21st CENTURY CLARINET SERIES

FOUR SHORT PIECES

Frank Bridge

Arranged for Clarinet and Piano by
Paula Corley

CLARINET

keisersouthernmusic.com

PERFORMANCE NOTES

Frank Bridge was born in February of 1879 in Brighton, England. He began his musical life as a violinist, at London's Royal College of Music. Later he switched to the viola and became known as a virtuoso on the instrument as well as a composer and teacher. His catalogue of works contains 192 compositions written between 1900 and 1941. One of his private composition students was Benjamin Britten with whom he maintained a close friendship. In 1939, shortly before his death, he gifted Britten with his Giussani viola.

Four Short Pieces was composed in 1912 and was originally written for violin or cello with piano. A number of recordings exist for these combinations as well as a version for flute and piano. This arrangement for clarinet and piano follows the original closely with regards to tempo, style and articulation. Markings are suggested and the performer is encouraged to make adjustments to facilitate musicality.

Ranges

Movement one, *Meditation*, is an elegant and lyrical ABA form that showcases the chalumeau and clarion register of the clarinet. The peaceful opening quickly changes to a more intense *piu mosso* at ms. 19 before ending quietly.

Spring Song is a quick, up-tempo melody in 2/4 that is reminiscent of a brisk walk or carriage ride in the English countryside. The style is legato and there are some large interval skips.

Lullaby is a slow waltz that requires good air support as the clarinetist must sustain with a beautiful sound throughout.

Country Dance is the most technically demanding of the movements in quick 6/8 time. The clarinetist must move fluidly through the full range of the instrument while creating the "dance" style through carefully placed agogic accents. The accents should be substantial, and both clarinetist and pianist should work for contrast when they appear.

Four Short Pieces

I. Meditation

Clarinet in B♭

Frank Bridge
arranged by Paula Corley

4

II. Spring Song

Frank Bridge
arranged by Paula Corley

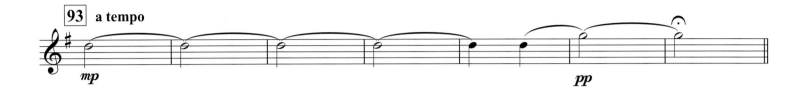

III. Lullaby

Frank Bridge
arranged by Paula Corley

6

IV. Country Dance

Frank Bridge
arranged by Paula Corley

43 **a tempo but slightly faster**

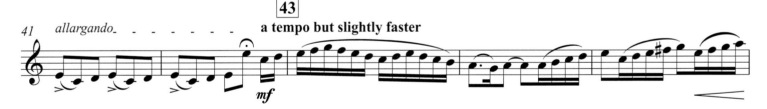

III. Lullaby

Frank Bridge
arranged by Paula Corley

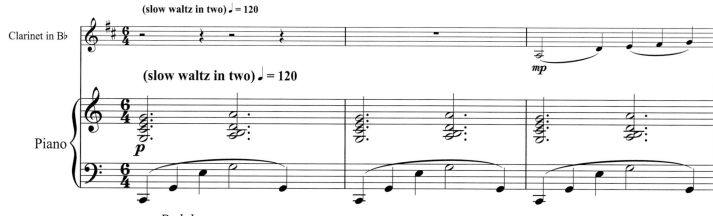

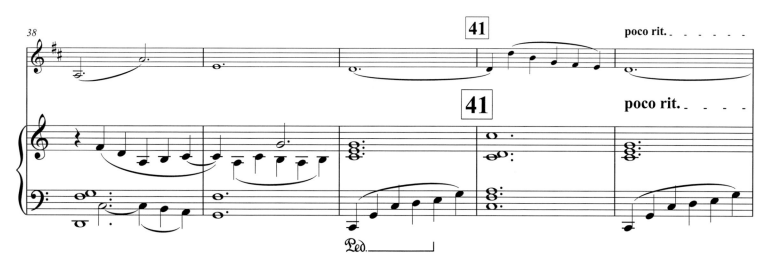

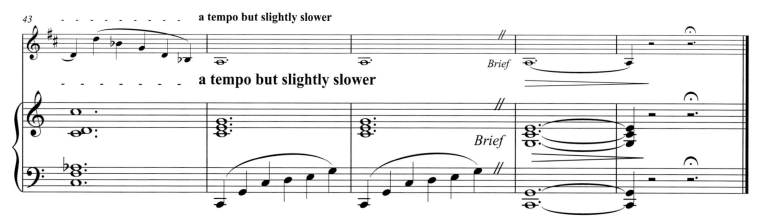

IV. Country Dance

Frank Bridge
arranged by Paula Corley